Reflections

A compilation of raw emotions on Life ,
Nature and human compassion

Nagarajan Pradeep

BookLeaf
Publishing

India | USA | UK

Made with ❤ on the BookLeaf Publishing Platform
www.bookleafpub.in
www.bookleafpub.com

Dedication

In loving memory of my parents
Nagarajan and Prema

Preface

This is a collection of my poems , starting from my teenage rumblings going through life phases of success, failure, Risk, Hope, Love, despair displaying varied raw emotions

I am an avid traveler and have my poetic feel of Nature and Wildlife about which I am very fond of. Life is all about living the moment and so also are my poems. I am sure you will enjoy it

Let me Dawn my writing journey with this beautiful Sanskrit verse

For yesterday is but a Dream and
Tomorrow is only a Vision
But today well lived makes
Every yesterday a Dream of Happiness and
Every Tomorrow a vision of Hope
Look well therefore to this day
Such is the salutation of Dawn.

Acknowledgements

Special thanks to my family members who had encouraged me to express myself

You are God

Ganesha-The beginner
We procrastinate to do things
You have to start –To learn, to evaluate, to do things
Any Beginning-You are Ganesha

Brahma –The Creator
We create our own lives
A New idea, A new solution
Any new creation-You are Brahma

Vishnu The Preserver
We show compassion to our fellow being
We help and support a person in need
Any act done with Love and without expectation-You are
Vishnu

Shiva-The Destroyer
We have Bad habits
Envy, Greed and Fear-They have to be destroyed
Any destruction of bad habits-You are Shiva

These are Life's principles
Start,
Do your own creation

Live with Compassion
Destroy Bad Habits
Live a Happy Life

2. My first Victory

The crowd was roaring
We were down by a Goal.
There were three minutes left
And we had to do something
Or we would lose.....
The word Lose was new to me
Soon the whistle was blown
And we lost.

As I left the field
Fighting to hold back the tears that filled my eyes
I felt some one pat my back and say
"Son when you lose, You lose alone".

Later when I failed to make the team
When my girl friend walked out of me
When I lost my job
When I lost and stood alone
His words floated to my mind

Every time I won and basked in the warmth of Victory
My thoughts went back to those who have lost
It was least I could do to make my victory complete

And pay homage to the kind old soul, who had taught
me How to lose.

3. Risk

To Laugh is to Risk appearing a fool
To weep is to Risk appearing sentimental
To reach out for another is to Risk involvement
To expose your feelings is to expose your true self
To Love is to Risk not being Loved in return
To Live is to Risk dying
To Hope is to Risk despair,
To Try at all is to Risk failure
But Risk, we must
Because the greatest hazard in Life is to risk nothing
The man who Risks nothing
He may avoid suffering....
But he simply cannot Learn, Feel, Change, Grow, Love or
Live.....
He has forfeited freedom.

4. My Life

I am-I am not
I know not what I am
I ponder upon the strangeness of my existence
Mortal or Immortal, Divinity or Evil I cannot say

My life is a paradox
Bubbling with joy one moment
Plumb into the depths of misery next moment
Superficial, Thoughtful, Elated, Miserable
That is what I am

I hear life is but a dream
Is it nightmare or ecstasy-A contradiction to be sure
For yet, I have not unraveled it
I know not when-If I will
My life is a question mark
I know not but I care

5. Secret of Success

That person is a success
Who has lived well, laughed often and loved much
Who has gained the respect of common man
And the love of children

That person is a success
Who enjoyed what he did
Who leaves the world better than he found it
Whether by a perfect poem or by a guiding thought

That person is a success
Who never lacked appreciation of earth's beauty
Who looked for the best in others
And gave the best he had

6. Nine to Fiver

I am a Nine to Fiver
Yes, which many long for
But I have a different tale to tell

I live in the ocean of humanity
Which races with time and space
My nest is a little larger than a solitary confinement cell
My morning starts with radio song and a quarrel for a
bucket of water

I see this beggar girl and the leper boy every day but
now my feelings are trimmed
When I passed them, I used to get a little disturbed
initially but not anymore
As I join the long queue for bus
I search for some new face and life in that herd of
humanity

The strikes, the firings and the deaths
The accidents, the rapes and the thefts
Many times, just indicate the presence of other human
beings
I consider them as unaccounted taxes we have to pay for
this civilized society

7. Hope

Tired and Lost-
Fighting alone the battle of Life
Against conflicts from within and without
Against people who don't even deserve to be my
enemies
Against the might of the spiteful
Against my failures and flaws
Against All odds
I am tired and lost

But not really
The rest is only for a while
For the day is not far off
When I am back with a smile
The battle continues
For there is the light of hope
That there are better days ahead.

8. The Will to do

If you can dream and not make the dream your master
If you can think and not make thought your aim
If you can meet with triumph and disaster
And treat these two imposters just the same

If you can force your heart, nerve and sinew
To serve your turn long after they are gone
And so, hold on when there is nothing in you
Except the will which says you to hold on

If you can fill the unforgiving minute
With sixty seconds worth of distance run
Yours is the earth and everything that's in it
And what's more, you will be man my son

9. The Power of Words

A careless word may kindle strife
A cruel word may wreck a life
A bitter word may instill hate
A brutal word may smite and kill

A gracious word may light the day
A timely word may lessen stress
A supportive word may induce confidence
A loving word may heal and bless

10. Don't Quit

When things go wrong, as they sometimes will
When the road you are trudging is all uphill
When the funds are low and the debts are high
And you want to smile but you only can sign
When stress is pressing you down a bit
Rest if you must, but don't you ever quit

Life is queer with its twists and turns
Don't give up though the pace seems slow
You may succeed with another blow
Success is failure turned inside out
So, stick to the fight when you are hardest hit
It's when things seem worst that you must not quit

11. Life's Paradox

Life's Paradox

Man comes into the world without his consent
He usually goes out of it against his will
Between these two events, his life is ruled by paradoxes

When he is little, big girls kiss him
When he grows up, only little girls kiss him

If he is poor, he is said to be a bad manager
If he is rich, he is suspected of dishonesty

If he is in politics, he takes bribes
If he is out of politics, he is not patriotic

If he gives it for charity, he does it for show
If he does not, he is a skinflint

If he is actively religious, he is a hypocrite
If he is not, he is a hardened sinner

If he shows affection, he is a softie
If he does not, he is cold blooded

If he saves money, he is miser
If he spends it, he is a spend thrift

So, what's the use
Never worry about what others think
Do what your conscience says

12. The many facets of Life

Enjoy the journey of Life

Life is a hidden message
Life is an unexplored passage
Life is an unsolved mystery
Life is an uneasy victory
Life is a brief beauty
Life is a sacred duty
Life is a daring adventure
Life is a tragic torture
Life is an incomplete journey
Life is an unextracted honey

In Life, Journey is more important than the destination

13. Our Leaders

Some are lean, some are fat
Some keep talking through their hat
Some issue statement's ,Ten a day
Some can't think of what to say
Some make millions along the way
Some can't find a single pie
Some strive to educate the masses
Some get lost in caste and classes
Some keep Left, some keep Right
Some change parties overnight
Some propagate spinning
Some wear dhotis and keep grinning
Some dream of our ancient civilization
With all these diverse political opinions
May the Lord have mercy on our dominions

14. Best things you can Give

The best things you can give

Forgiveness for your enemies
Tolerance to your opponents
Good Heart to your friend
Small appreciation to people you interact daily

Respect for your father
Good conduct for your mother
support for your spouse
Good Example to your children

Above all
Self-respect for yourself
Generosity to people at large
Care for the flora and fauna and enjoy this beautiful
world

15. Softness and Gentleness are companions of Life

When a person is born, he is tender and weak
At Death, he is hard and stiff

When plants are alive, they are soft and supple
When they are dead, they are brittle and dry

Hardness and stiffness are companions of death
Softness and gentleness are companions of Life

The big and strong belong underneath
The gentle and subtle raise to the Top

16. Whispering Hopes

When I let my thoughts break free
Breaking the rules and conception of morality
They float softly across the dark sky
Or break over the bright city lights

Someone somewhere is waiting for me
How much longer is this wait to be
It is hard work to carry on alone
With no one to acknowledge what you have done

No doctorates to wave off, No Titles do I bear
Only winning small battles- to be just, to be fair
I feel beautiful each time I win
Proud of myself, I thrust out my chin

Then there are times, I feel lonely in a crowd
"Where was it all leading to?", I silently shout
But how can I surrender, when I still believe
That some one somewhere is still waiting for me

17. Living the moment

He is born
Grows up in a neatly defined society
He conforms to set patterns or perhaps rebels
He caters to the whims of intellect and emotions

He confirms to the cliques in which he exists
Sometimes anguished to make both ends meet
Sometimes languishing in idle luxury
He lives in a ready made world

Orbiting on Ego trips
Sometimes compromising
He drifts generally entangled in ties of kinship
Each so well defined by his community

He finally just disappears
From the cosmos which was always there
Why then does he take the existence so seriously
Life is all about living the moment.

18. The Boring Lecturer

Time
Hangs heavy on his hands, as he enters the class
He is aware of his in competence to teach
But he is too smart to let you discover that

Blame him not
After all, he did not opt for the job
He wanted to be someone else
So now, he dwells on trivialities
Encourages debates and confusions
And nit picking

As long as you are distracted
By discussions protracted
And do not catch on to know
That he knows nothing

Nothing is lost
Except
Time

19. Adolescence

I am too old to be young
Too young to be old
I am an adolescent

When I am assertive, I am insolent
If I am not, I am lacking in drive
When I make my own decisions, I am too big for my
boots
If I don't, I am still so immature
I am too old to be tied to Mamma's apron strings
Too young to be left to fend for myself

I need counsel
I need guidance
I need help to be a better me
I am at the cross roads of my life
I am, you see
Just an Adolescent

20. Freedom for Expressing your love

I read the great poems, the classic poems, the poems that dealt with love
I experienced love quite late
And found it not as romantic as I have read

For when I fell in love
She said I had no right to love
Don't I have a right for my own emotion

Am I not allowed to express my emotion
But when I said I am in love
She said I have no right

Well, I could have said
I have a right to love
You have a right to deny

But you know, love is a complicated emotion
I kept silent, wondering
Whether one has the right to express one's own emotion

21. Sky Diving

We arrived at the isolated airstrip
The small aircraft standing along
Mind filled with adrenaline but body tense with fear
We put on the jump suit
The instructor tells the process
Here we Go

The Plane climbs up
We see vast space of deserts and small human dwellings
The clouds go past us and life becomes too small
In the vast space, I sit cramping
The mind is blank and desolate
Waiting for the inevitable

Here goes the free fall
You are falling like a stone from fifteen thousand feet
You are flashing your hands like wings
The biggest life risk is taken
The fall is breathtaking adrenaline
You know you exist

The Earth below you seem vast
The desert and the sea look incredibly beautiful
You seem floating amidst clouds in vast sky

You spin upside down alternating between earth and sky
The air is gushing like you are caught amidst a storm
The law of gravitation holds

The chute is opened
You see the world in a bird's eye view
How small the world and how high you are
The speed of fall is slow and you screech to your heart
content
Nobody can hear but you
The landscape slowly becomes big
You slowly land on the beach

Sky diving teaches you to fly, fall and land
Sky diving makes you fearless
Sky diving makes you resilient
Sky diving makes you see the world in different
perspective
Sky diving is a rebirth
You are not the same person again

22. Strength and confidence

The majestic posture
The forever alertness
The power of speed
All are to be learned from a Cheetah

The perseverance to lift objects beyond their weight
The agility of a fast climb into huge trees
The power of solitariness
All are to be learned from a Leopard

The Dominance
The relaxed hunt
The power of group in prides
All are to be learned from a Lion

The raw strength
The self-confident walk into any situation
The power of resilience
All are to be learned from a Tiger

The ambition to leap forward
The aquatic power to swim against currents
The power of elegance
All are to be learned from a Jaguar

The elegance and simplicity
The ability to wither harsh terrains
The power of big leap
All are to be learned from a Puma

Cheetah, leopard, lion, Tiger, Jaguar and puma
They may be different cat species with unique skills
They display casual dominance
 They symbolize strength and confidence

23. Snowfall

The snow comes down white and weightless
The snow is falling on the ground
Piling in enormous mounds
Makes the fields, lake and all landscape silvery
I see a dream white world
I feel the wet snow
On my warm dry skin
So pure, so white, the most beautiful creation
Words cannot describe this sensation

I relish the freezing moments of my life
The night is glittering white
The snow flake is a master piece
The dark clouds show myriad images
The Gentle breeze is shivering my spine
Thoughts go on in my mind

I see the tall snow-covered Pines
That tell of survival and growth by persistence
I see also the leafless winter trees
That tell winter is temporal phase
I will grow brim in Summer

I remember Robert Frosts Lines

The Woods are lovely, dark and deep
But I have promises to keep
And miles to go before I sleep

24. Memories

Memories like solitary islands
float along my sea of thoughts
Sometimes I stoop to gather...
Long forgotten dreams...
Buried hopes....
The links of my youth
The waves turn stormy...
And my mind protests in pain
Then reflection of happier times
Shimmer in the horizon
Beckon towards recollection of joy
And I rush to capture the fragile moments
So much has gone
So much is still to be
Even as I think
The ebb and flow of the tides
Casts a spell of forgetfulness
And the waters grow calm again..

25. Horse Riding

MAX, the name of my horse
the brown one with long hair and
long feet, flying without wings,
Hop on his back for a ride
We go together in the Beach
Our bond is special
the beautiful sea
the crashing waves;
the small boats seen distantly
the gentle breeze
the rising sun,
the colourful sky
All provide a nice ambience for my Horse Ride
Sitting perfectly upright,
joyful and relaxed,
Boots in the stirrups
I hold on both hands
loosely, the reins of my Horse:
Kicking gently
Excitement bubbling up in me
As I learn how to trot
Up and down,up and down
My body smoothly raising off the saddle
I begin enjoying my ride.

The ride was wonderful, we really had a blast,
Horse riding is truly an experience
It brings us the contact with rare element of grace,
beauty and an insatiable spirit
It is an emotional experience of a beautiful bond
between a man and a Horse

26. Sea Kayaking

Moving with the waves
Started off turbulently to tranquil water
Means turbulence in the near and calm in the far
That is what Life is all about

Moving with the waves
Floating in the depths of fifty meters
Seeing the pelicans perching in the ridges
Makes one abandon fear

Moving with the waves
Seeing the waves crashing the Rocks
Spawning through one hundred falls
Make one wonder Natures beauty

Moving with the waves
Drenched in the golden sunshine at dawn
Seeing the mountains far behind
Makes us realize how small we are

Moving with the waves
Grazing through the weeds
Seeing the odd Cape Seal
Make one understand the meaning of existence

Moving with the waves
Floating over huge waves
Seeing the odd baby whale
Makes one understand calmness in turbulence

Moving with the waves
Fresh cool breeze blowing through the seas
Cormorants and Sea gulls' lullabies in the sky
Makes one realize what serenity is all about.

27. Kitten Poetry

Each morning, I awake,
my pet cat my child is beside me,
his eyes are wide with love,
and my heart brims with delight
Each morning, I keep food for my other pets
my pet cat my child is beside me,
his body circling my legs
Follows me wherever I go
Each evening, I watch Television
my pet cat my child is in my lap
I cuddle and caress him
He sleeps on my lap
On some nights when I am late from work
my pet cat whines and greets even in midnight
He takes me inside home and
He says goodnight and goes out
He is very special,
a truly amazing soul,
he is very soft and gentle,
forever a loving cat

28. What I want the World Leaders to strive for

Let us eliminate discrimination based on caste and creed
Let us stop bigotry based on religion and nationality
Let us not engage in killing a large group of people in
the name of war
Let us learn to Love and respect human life.

Let us eliminate killing Rhinos and Elephants for profit
Let us stop murdering animals in the name of hunting
for Trophies
Let us not butcher wild animals in the name of Bush
meat and delicious food
Let us learn to Love and respect Wildlife.

Let us eliminate felling huge trees and construct mega
dams in the name of development.
Let us stop deforestation
Let us not engage in mass urbanization by damaging
environment
Let us learn to Love and respect forests and wilderness.

Let us eliminate Famine
Let us stop malnutrition
Let us not use pesticides and harm our food products.

Let us learn to Love and provide healthy food to all
humans.

Let us work to eliminate killer diseases like Carona,
cancer, AIDS, Alzheimer's with better knowledge
Let us stop infant deaths with effective vaccination
Let us not engage in making money on common man's
health
Let us learn to Love and give affordable healthcare to all

Let us work to eliminate global warming
Let us reduce greenhouse gas emissions
Let us not engage in increasing fossil fuel support and
look for clean energy sources
Let us learn to love and respect the environment

Let us eliminate our ignorance of the Universe with
better knowledge
Let us stop pretending that we know everything about
the Universe
Let us not engage in destructive activities and reduce our
life in the universe
Let us learn to Love and be humble that we are a very
miniature part of Milky way Galaxy

Let us not work to being FIRST
Let us stop our wrong doings to Our People, Forests,

Wildlife and Environment
Let us eradicate hunger, famine, diseases and work
towards good health for all
Let us learn to Love and Dignity to all Living things be
our motto

29. All things of Nature are Free

All things of Nature are free
Live the Life you Love.
Love the Life you Live.
That is what Life is all about.

The majestic mountains
The pristine Forests and massive Savannah
The sandy deserts and desolate beaches
This is what Life is all about.

The hovering bees
The chirping birds
The Grazing animals in morning dew
This is what Life is all about.

The rising sun and the warmth of dawn
The beautiful moon with its varied shape as per season
The twinkling stars and colorful skies
That is what Life is all about.

The gentle breeze and flowing streams
The big trees and dense bushes

The roaring waves and sand dunes
That is what life is all about

Mother Earth with its blissful beauty
Majestic sun lighting the day
Serene water showing the way
That is what Life is all about

Live the Life you Love
Love the Life you Live
Live for the moment and keep moving
That is what Life is all about

30. My Daughters

I looked at you when you were born,
and knew then straight away the joy of Life had begun
You came into my world, so tiny and so small...
And I was in awe to watch you grow and play.
You bring to me a heart of joy and memories so great,
and a powerful sense of fatherhood that no one can
debate.
I have seen you run and jump and shout and calling out
my name.
No love that I have ever known could ever feel the same.
The next few years will so quickly fly,
You'll always be my source of pride
You must stand up tall and proud, within you feel no
fear,
For all you dream and goals sit before you very near.
I have lived with you through the years to see you laugh,
cry and grow...
And it is difficult to know that someday I will have to let
you go.
And so my little princess before you go to sleep,
Remember I am your daddy and I am always yours to
keep

31. Amazon Rain Forest

Lush green vegetation with tall canopies, shrubs,
creepers with no pathways
Even Sun finds its rays hard to enter
Amazon, the Lungs of the Earth,
I was awestruck by its splendor.

Cool morning breeze, blazing sun, torrential rain
Swirling wind and cold nights
Amazon has all seasons in a single day
Makes you wonder why you should wait to see season
 for the whole year

Swimming in crystal clear waters with Dolphins and
Caimans
Canoeing in the ever-winding streams to see its amazing
birds
Long walks on unknown paths and get lost in wilderness
Amazon is heaven on earth

Monkeys howling in the trees
Flocks of Parrots and Macaws in clay licks
Toucans touching the sky and Spoon bills spawning the
water
Amazon has half the species of wildlife of the globe

The majestic ceiba Tree, the aguaje palm swamps
Walking along the creek amidst the dangerous stingrays
Seeing the lazy capybara on the way
Hearing the sounds of Amazon in all its splendor

The morning walk is like in an oven, with sweat beads
flowing through my body
I see am amazing array of bird at Dawn, the Arcadis,
parrots and Jades
The night walk is in cold breeze with jackets on to see
many insects and scorpions
The gushing river with jungle sounds, Amazon is forever
to cherish

32. Dawn

The misty morning sky
The cool breeze
The colorful sun rays
All say Dawn has arrived

The chirping of the birds
The whistling of the sparrow
The singing of the parrot
All say dawn has arrived

The squeaks of the squirrel
The cooing of the mynah
The fluttering of the dove
All say dawn has arrived

The aura of the fresh air
The beautiful trees with dew drops
The warmth of the daybreak
All say dawn has arrived

The mind seizes the present moment
The moment of sweet sounds
The vision of the enfolding day
Makes me fresh for the day

Everyday has a different shade
Everyday has a different melody
Everyday has a different weather
Makes me enjoy each day

33. Death of a Dog

Loving and loyal,
 Affectionate to the core,
 We were delighted with your puppy cuddles
 and watched you grow into the protective kid.

She walked with me wherever I go for eight long years
fast, alert, wary of any strange things and protective of
us
I had no fears, I know she is there, If danger comes from
anywhere
She loved our family with conditions none and treated us
like a special one.

You bring me peace with your head on my lap
I gently stroked your pure fur
Lovingly I bend to caress your forehead and friendly kick
box when you leap
I miss these moments for the rest of my life

There'll be no one to bark
 When any outsider comes by.
 It's going to be one of those moments
 When I'm sure I'll want to cry.
May your soul rest in Peace

34. War

History is full of Wars
War has produced Heroes and conquests
War is about Victor and vanquished
But War kills humans

The cause of war is forgotten
The cause of vanquished is forgotten
The treachery and cunningness of Valor is called tactics
War creates misery to vanquished

The cause of war is lust for women
The cause of war is craving for wealth
The cause of war is necrophilia and killing of person
War creates lust, wealth and group euphoria

The destruction of kingdom and economy is huge
The life of mass tortures, humiliation and rapes can't be
lived
The hatred of one group over the other is phenomenal
War is destruction and absence of dignified life for
vanquished

Let us avoid the shrill of war
Let us work for development of the country

Let us avoid mass euphoria of war
Let us work for development of the society

35. Water

Water cleanses the body
Water cools the body
Water relishes the body
Relax and do bathing everyday

Water exercises the muscles
Water regulates your breathing
Water emboldens to explore what is underneath it
Relax and do swimming

Water allows cool breeze
Water makes us appreciate the beauty of lotus
Water flexes our muscles
Relax and do Boating

The gentle waves heals our legs with salt
Walking on sand strengthens our legs
The dawn and dusk are a beauty to see
Relax and do Beach walking

Bathing, Swimming, Boating and Beach walking
Are good exercises for everyone
Are natures exercises of enjoyment
Practice it and enjoy your life

36. God's own Country

Congo is God's own country
Blessed with nature and a unique wildlife
It is World's cradle of civilisation where humanity
evolved
Echoes of a world so deep, In the Congo's arms, we leap

Congo is a Monkey Land
The Patas, Ascanius and Mangabeys,
The Mitis, Galago's, and Guenons
The origin of species happened here

Congo is Great Apes Home land where humans evolved
The majestic Gorillas
The charming chimpanzees and
The intelligent Bonobos

Congo has distinctive wildlife found nowhere in the
world
The forest elephants, Bongos and Sitatungas
The Okapis, Duikers and dwarf buffaloes
We need to go deep in the jungle to have a glimpse of
them

Congo has majestic rivers and huge lakes

In jungle depths the time stands still,
The canopy, alive with nature's sound with many
undiscovered herbs
To cure humanity's ills

The symphony of parrots and birds at dawn
The dense forest with torrential rain is a natures delight
Amidst the vast expanse, in gentle breeze I wonder
I am blessed to be in Congo-A heaven on earth

37. Gardening

Gardening is a beauty
The budding flowers
The beautiful butterflies
The many shaped tadpoles
Makes you appreciate beauty in all its splendor

The changing season
The changing colours and rapid growth
Makes you appreciate reward for patience
Makes you appreciate changes in life

Gardening needs removal of weeds
Cutting and pruning of Plants
Make all plants get enough sunlight
Makes one learn of sharing and compassion

Gardening is an activity
Activity of tenacity and beauty
Activity of creation and preservation
Activity that bears flowers and fruits

38. Death

Death is a reality
All living persons will be dead some day
It is more important how we take care before the death
Less important, the death rituals

A person's memory is cherished
A peaceful prayer for departed soul
That is what we can do to the dead
We do not know what lies beyond.

Death due to old age is peaceful to the soul
Death by accident is painful the family
Life course of the family changes
The next in helm have to take responsibility for the
family

Life of budding stars have changed because of death in
family
From stability they were pushed to survival mode
Planning for succession is a must
Let us do it so that the next generation do not suffer

Death is a reality
Ritual is a formality

Hatred, enmity and past misdeeds should not be spoken
Remembrance and good memories should be spoken

Let us pay tribute to the departed soul
Love and affection should be the theme
Pleasant memories should be the theme
Continuing family relationship should be the theme

39. The Indian Monsoon

The sight of white, Grey and Dark clouds
The feel of approaching of the cloud
The slow speed of going from drop to drenched rain
This is Indian Monsoon

Water Here, there and everywhere
Water falls sliding on Hill slopes
Water flowing across the deserted landscapes
This is Indian Monsoon

The torrential rain is a beautiful sight
The buildings become waterfalls
The roads become lakes
Welcome the Monsoon

The stream crossing is flooded
We are greeted with the aura of fresh air
Drenching in rain is a pleasure
Welcome the monsoon

The trees look lush and green
The streams are in spate
The Deer's hide in the bush and peacock dance
Welcome the monsoon

Greenery here, there, every where
Animals enjoying fodder and water
Brown patch turn greener
Welcome the Monsoon

I am caught amidst the cows
People running hither and tither happily
The life is beautiful
Welcome the monsoon

The monsoon ushers in life in the Desert
The monsoon ushers in beauty to behold
The monsoon gives water for the year
This is Indian Monsoon

40. I want to be Unique

I have the burning desire to do something in life
Nothing too wonderful mind you
Like running the country or being the first person to
land on Mars
Just little things which to you are trivial and easy reach

I would like to start a business
Something small scales will do
Just to prove my elder brother
That I can be as enterprising as him

I would like to drive a car in the rally
Join a mountain trekking troupe
May be take up still photography
I really love the hang of it

I would like to direct a stage play
and act on it too
I know I can do justice
To any role I am called on to do

I would like to do something
Besides being a government clerk or a bank employee
So many options are open these days

But sad to say that closed door of the old world is still
hard to budge

58

41. The African Odessey

Life is staying in wilderness amidst sounds of the forest
in Okavango delta, Botswana
Life is to see brief moment between Life and death to see
lion pack in pursuit of Buffalo in Okavango
Life is to see amazing cheetahs busy amidst pack of
giraffes and huge herds of buffaloes in Savuti
Life is to see Elephants and Buffaloes swim in the huge
Chobe River
Life is to see thousands of impalas and baboons happily
co-exist in the same terrain in Chobe.

Life is walking in South Luangwa, Zambia to see the
venomous puff adder
Life is seeing a big lion pride relaxing with its beautiful
nine lion cubs
Life is seeing huge pack of wild dogs in the amazing
wilderness of its jungle
Life is walking in the night to see the elusive Leopard
and civets walking past you.
Life is to see majestic hippos graze in the night

Life is to see Leopard, cheetah so close in Ruaha,
Tanzania
Life is to visit the Hyena den to see mother Hyena with

her cubs
Life is seeing the majestic Ruaha river with hippos and
crocs
Life is about an elephant baby running to you and
blessing you by patting your head in your Land Rover.
Life is to see the rocky, riverine, savannah, wooded and
hilly terrain with its varied wildlife

Life is to climb the majestic Simien mountains, in
Ethiopia
Life is to sleep in top of four thousand meters in rustic
tent with subzero temperature amidst cold rains.
Life is hiding in a cave to see snow storm go past you.
Life is to go to panoramic imet gogo amidst its huge
cliffs and panoramic view where only eagles dare.
Life is to learn to ride on a mule and know about its
endurance.

Life is to visit the god forsaken Danakil Depression,
Ethiopia
Life is to swim in Afar Lake amidst its healthy hot water
springs.
Life is walking into the mouth of Erta hale volcano to see
its amazing eruptions and sleep there
Life is to swim in the deep Salt Lake which lifts you
automatically due to saline content
Life is to see colorful Dallol springs pouring water in

your head with fifty degrees temperature.

Life is not about existence and it is living the moment in this amazing nature.

42. Joy-Part 1

What is Joy?
Joy is all about doing
Joy is all about caring
Joy is all about daring
Joy is all about Loving
Joy is all about sharing

Joy in doing
A job well done.
An improvement in anything over yesterday.
Learning new things.
Taking responsibility for failures.
Sharing with team the success.

Joy in caring
Cuddling and caressing your pet.
See your sampling grow into majestic trees.
Caring for people around you in need.
Buying from small vendors than super markets.
Watching small acts of care wherever you go.

Joy is daring
Walking with Lions and cheetahs.
Sky diving from fifteen thousand feet.

Sea kayaking in two hundred feet amidst huge waves

Long trek to beautiful places.

Going to earth 's nadir to see its majestic splendour.

Joy is Loving

Enjoying affection and care of my lovely daughters.

Love and responsibility for my family.

Support for relatives in need.

Blessings of elders on occasions.

Meeting with friends on selection.

Joy is sharing

Sharing your knowledge with youngsters to make them think.

Sharing your experience so that others don't make same mistake.

Sharing right attitudes for happiness.

Sharing and doing acts of human compassion.

Sharing and being part of anything to do with human dignity.

Do,Care,Dare,Love, Share

Enjoy your Life

43. Joy Part 2

What is joy
The sound of bird at dusk
The sound of drizzling rain
The sound of playing children
The sound of old melodies in midnight
I am blessed with all

What is joy
The sight of sun rising at dawn
The sight of a varied garden
The sight of our elegant relatives on Occasions
The sight of acts of compassion on the roads
I am blessed with all

What is joy
The smell of a fragrant flower
The smell of honeycomb in the garden
The smell of sand before the drizzle
The smell of favorite dish under preparation
I am blessed with all

What is joy
The taste of a sumptuous dinner
The taste of a roadside ice cream

The inner taste of a lovely poem
The inner taste of a beautiful piece of art
I am blessed with all

What is joy
The warm greetings and hugs of your dear ones on
occasions
The caressing of your dog every time it meets you
The shouting and dancing of our dear ones on occasions
The playing of children irrespective of occasions
I am blessed with all

What is joy
The chit chatting of my lovely daughters
The caring of my pets
The ambience of my garden
The Love and care of my near and dear ones
I am blessed with all

Joy is daily
Joy is occasional
Joy is seasonal
The type of joy varies
More importantly joy is from with in
Relish it

44. Sailing in the Atlantic Ocean

We went into the Atlantic Ocean at day break
The Sea gulls flying and swimming
The silent sea greeting the colorful sun
The lazy waves, the gentle breeze
We went deep into the Atlantic for a calm retreat

The Cape fur Seals, the gentle giants came into the boat
They played,they posed
We cuddled them, We caressed them
They jumped, they slept with us and went back to the
Ocean
It was an amazing feel

We visited the Seal colonies with thousands of Seals
The small island amidst the gentle waves
The baby seals playing and swimming under the
watchful eyes of their mother
Each family having a separate space
It was a beautiful community living

We sailed through Flamingo colony
They swam, they flew and came to us
They played, they posed

They had their share of eat
It was delight to watch them in their colonies

We went further down in the Ocean
We saw the beauty of Dolphins swimming
The occasional breaches
The verdant chases
It was Nature's beauty at its best

The Atlantic Ocean in Walvis Bay
The occasional ship wreck, the far-off land
The amazing Dolphins, Seals, Pelicans and Seagulls
Amidst calm sea with gentle breeze in morning sun
Makes sailing a Heaven on Earth

45. The Living Desert

We arrived at the living desert
Sands with shades of gravel, white and brown
The gentle breeze blowing
Walking on sand was like being in a dream
The feeling was awesome

We saw lizards, chameleons, beetles and snakes
We saw Welwitschia, Lithops, Hoodia, Nara Melon and
Quivers
We saw desert not as barren land
It was living and full of life
We were amazed by the mid-day treasures

The absorbing of winter dew by plants
Antelopes like Addax, springboks and Oryx feeding on
plants
Hyenas and Jackals completing the food chain of the
desert
We understood how food chains work in remote deserts
We were amazed by its versatility

The varied size of the dunes
The changing dunes at dawn, noon, dusk and night
The cliffs and the Valleys

The ecstasy of sliding, jumping and falling on the sand
It was nature caressing us with the sun, Moon and stars

The far view of the sea
The crashing waves with the gentle breeze
The majestic dunes with piercing sun
The amazing silence amidst the sounds of nature
Swakopmund is living desert with amazing life and feel.

46. The South American enigma

Life is going into wilderness amidst Uyuni salt flats,
Bolivia with Mirror Effect
Life is walk amidst Fumaroles with steaming sands in
cold subzero temperature and howling winds.
Life is taking bath in the Hot springs facing the Volcano
and desert
Life is to see the Red Lagoon, Green Lagoon, White
Lagoon and Black Lagoon with contrasting fauna
Life is to see the Incahausi island with giant cactus
amidst desert, huge mountains and Volcanoes

Life is Hiking the Torres Del Paine National Park, Chile
with its majestic glaciers and flowing streams
Life is seeing the majestic pumas and free roaming
horses in the amazing steppes
Life is to horse ride at Lake Nordenskjold with its
picturesque green water amidst imposing glaciers
Life is about tiring hike to Mirador las Torres, the park's
three distinctive granite peaks.
Life is to see majestic Grey Glacier with massive icebergs
floating and cold waves in Pebble beach

Life is trekking the amazing Tambopata Reserve, Peru

the most bio diverse place in the Planet
Life is to see clay licks where Macaws and parakeets
flock in thousands to lick clay for minerals
Life is to see hundreds of birds -Macaws, Guans, Trogons
, Blue Jays, Jacamars singing their melody
Life is about seeing Monkeys jumping, iguanas lazing
and Anaconda's resting in the massive jungle
Life is to see Caimans, Tapirs and Capybaras lazing in
Amazon river with elusive jaguar watching

Life is trekking the Monteverde Cloud forest , Costa
Rica he jewel in the crown of cloud forests
Life is to embrace the misty atmosphere, to observe
plants , orchids ,ferns and copious wildlife.
Life is about The El Tigre walk amidst waterfalls, endless
cascades and rickety swing bridges.
Life is about going down to Murchilego falls and having
a relishing swim
Life is about seeing butterflies, Sloths, Monkeys and
array of birds amidst clouds and cascades

Life is trekking the Cano Crystales, the rainbow river of
Columbia
Life is canoeing into Guayabero river at sunrise amidst
Dolphins , Iguanas and morning Bird lullabies
Life is hike amidst water, rocks, pebbles,Sand in the
colorful river-blue, green, yellow, red and orange

Life is to climb steep and roll across slopes., walking in
knee deep water in its magnificent colors
Life is tiring the body but with fresh heart swimming
and bathing in the beautiful scenery unfolding

Life is not about existence and it is living the moment in
this amazing nature.

47. My Love

When I think of her sparkling face
And of her body that rocked this way and that way

When I think of her laughter
Her jubilance that filled me
It is a wonder; I have not gone mad

She is away and I cannot do what I want
Other faces pale when I get close on

She is away and I cannot breathe her in
Her wholeness I know to be a fiction of my making

Still, I cannot dismiss the longing for her
It is a craving for sensation of a new flesh that cannot
wholly calm me
It is perhaps far more than her

48. Breakup

Our weeks of Love
Passed like gently trotting horses
There were off days
Days of cold gloom
Lost in blank doubt

Unlike others
She would never forget or forgive
Wallowing in self-pity
Looking for apologies for ever
Of course it would have to end in sweet agony

I had no time for rules and conventions
For I would become free again
Smelling the spring and jumping fences
Trotting in the sun shine and kissing in the rain
I am a Happy man

49. A Day in Masai Mara

Here is a day in Masai Mara for you
The ever-expanding Savannah with flowing rivers, ponds
and hillocks
With huge herds of Antelopes -Gazelles, Impalas,
Hartebeest's and Topi's
The gentle walking Giraffe with their calf
The migrating Gnu's and Zebras in huge herds

Here is the big five
The majestic lion pride relaxing in the wild
The leopard on a tree and Black Rhino on the run
The intelligent elephants in huge herds
Huge herds of Buffaloes in the many marshy ponds

Here is the special five of the Mara
The majestic cheetah coalition
The huge pods of Hippos in Mara and Talek River
The giant night crocodile always alert seeking its prey
The busy ostrich perching the ground and Vultures
airing around

Mara brims with wildlife- Here, there, every where
The noisy baboons
The ever-busy wart hogs

The constant moving jackals in pairs
Hyenas on the hunt and in the den

Mara is always special
There is Mongoose in and out of their burrows
The elusive Elands and Dik Dik's sneaking in
The singing birds, the poisonous pythons and many
other species unheard of
All you may see in a single day

50. The Himalayas

I went there by chance
I met her by chance
We became one by chance
And yet, many a time, I have wondered
Was it really a chance

There were Slopes and Slopes
Some barren, some snow capped
Some filled with those tall straight pines
But as I walked on them picking untrodden paths
Little did I know that it was here, I will find my heart

Everywhere that I went
A silence filled my soul
The trees whispered to me
The birds' chirping filled my ear
The flowing streams sung the melody

I would run down a slope
Or trudge up a hillock
I would walk into the flowing streams and waterfalls
I would sit down in silence on the nature's lawn
Or burst into a lullaby

Whatever I did
Wherever I went
Whenever I looked
She was always there hand in hand with me
She is my love for the mountains

51. Measure of Man

A man is not measured by the Titles, however high
sounding it may be
Not by the marks or Rank, he got in his professional
degrees
Not by the social rank or Award by cliché group
Not by the earthly pomp and show displaying the wealth
possessed

He is measured by his justice right
His fairness at his play
His squareness in all the dealings made
His Honest upright ways

These are the measures ever there to serve him when
they can
For Man is no bigger than the way he treats his fellow
men.

52. Take time

Take Time to Live, convert moments to memories
Take time to work, it is building of Experience for future success
Take time to think, it is the source of your power
Take time to play, it is the fountain of wisdom
Take time to dream, it is hitching your wagon to the star
Take time to be friendly, it is a road to happiness
Take time to look around, it is too short a day to be selfish
Take time to laugh, it is the music of the soul
Take time to play with Children, it is the joy of joy
Take time to be courteous, it is the mark of a gentleman